MOTORCYCLES
COLORING BOOK

I0414321

free download coloring pages

At : bit.ly/get_sample_free

V Art Studio

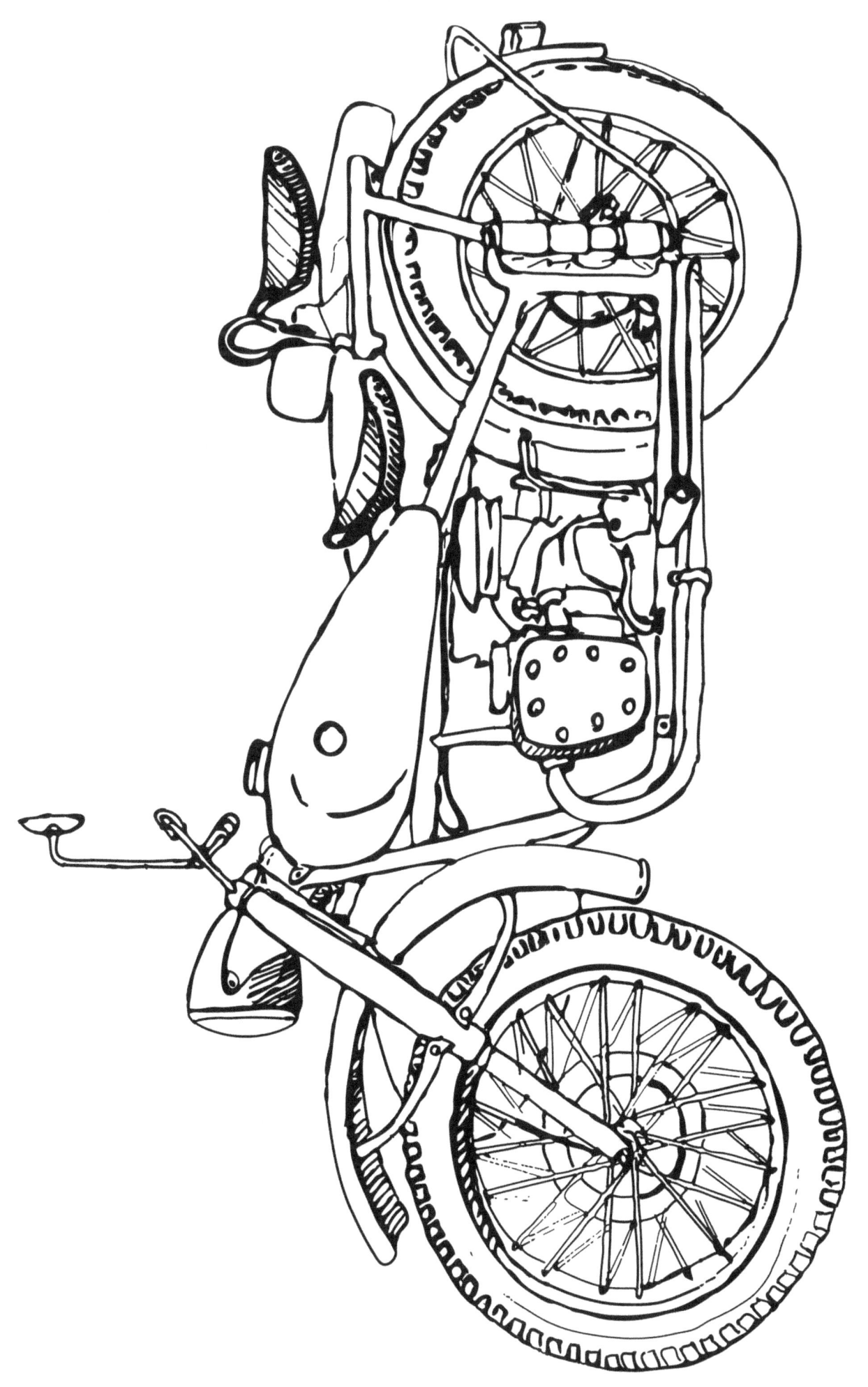

Follow your heart!

American

Motor

Riders Club

Live Fast Die Young

Keep your bike in
GOOD REPAIR:
MOTORCYCLE BOOTS
ARE NOT COMFORTABLE
for walking

CUSTOM

MOTORCYCLES

BORN TO RIDE

VINTAGE CUSTOM MOTORCYLES

California

◆1976◆

UNION SUPPLY CO.

RIDE LIKE THE WIND
LEGENDARY RIDERS
SUPER BUILT FOR SPEED POWER
IRON WHEELS
SUPERIOR PERFORMANCE

old school motorcycles

Since **Club** 1963

Retro Bikes

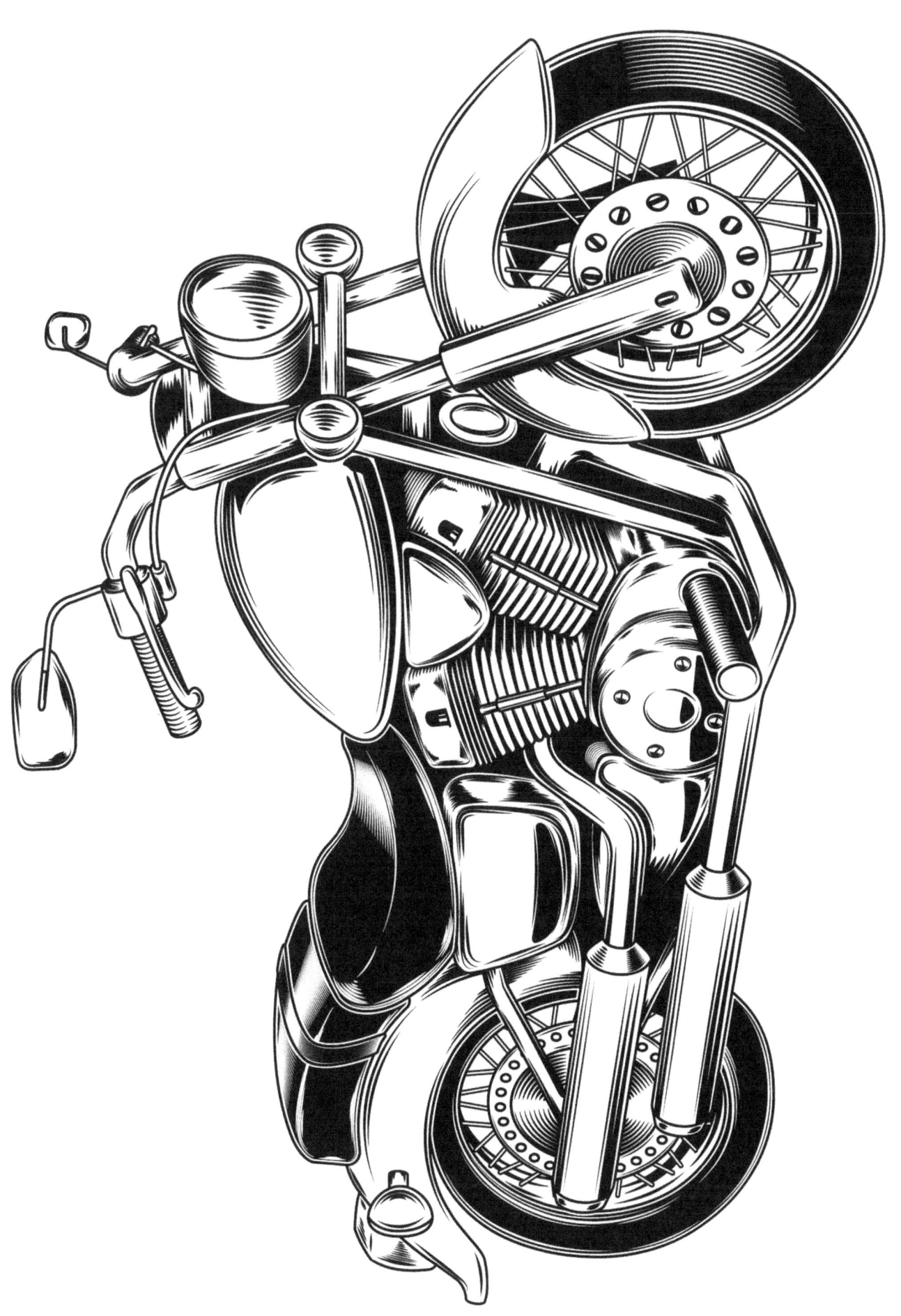

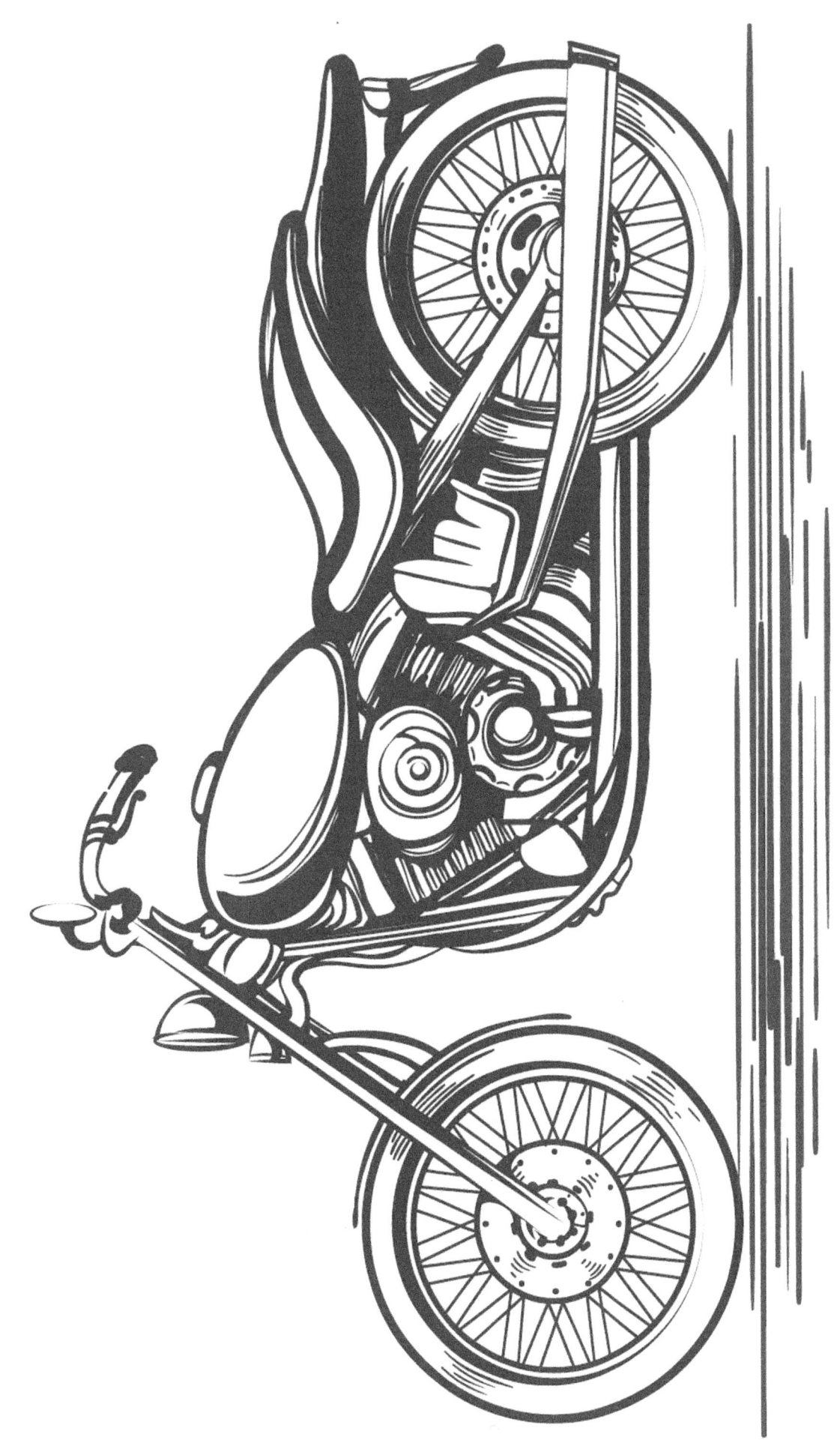

let the weekend begin

CUSTOM MADE

CHOPPERS

19 87

NEW YORK

AMERICAM DREAM

HIGH QUALITY APPARELS COMPANY

MOTORCYCLE

ENDLESS GOOD TIMES

Cafe Racer
Garage
Custom
HAND MADE PROJECT

100%
Guaranteed
Quality

ORIGINAL QUALITY

CALIFORNIA

Vintage Motorcycle

Great Team

LEGEND

RIDERS

85

SUPERIOR PERFORMANCE

★ LEGENDARY ★

CLASSIC BIKERS CLUB

Ride Like The Wind

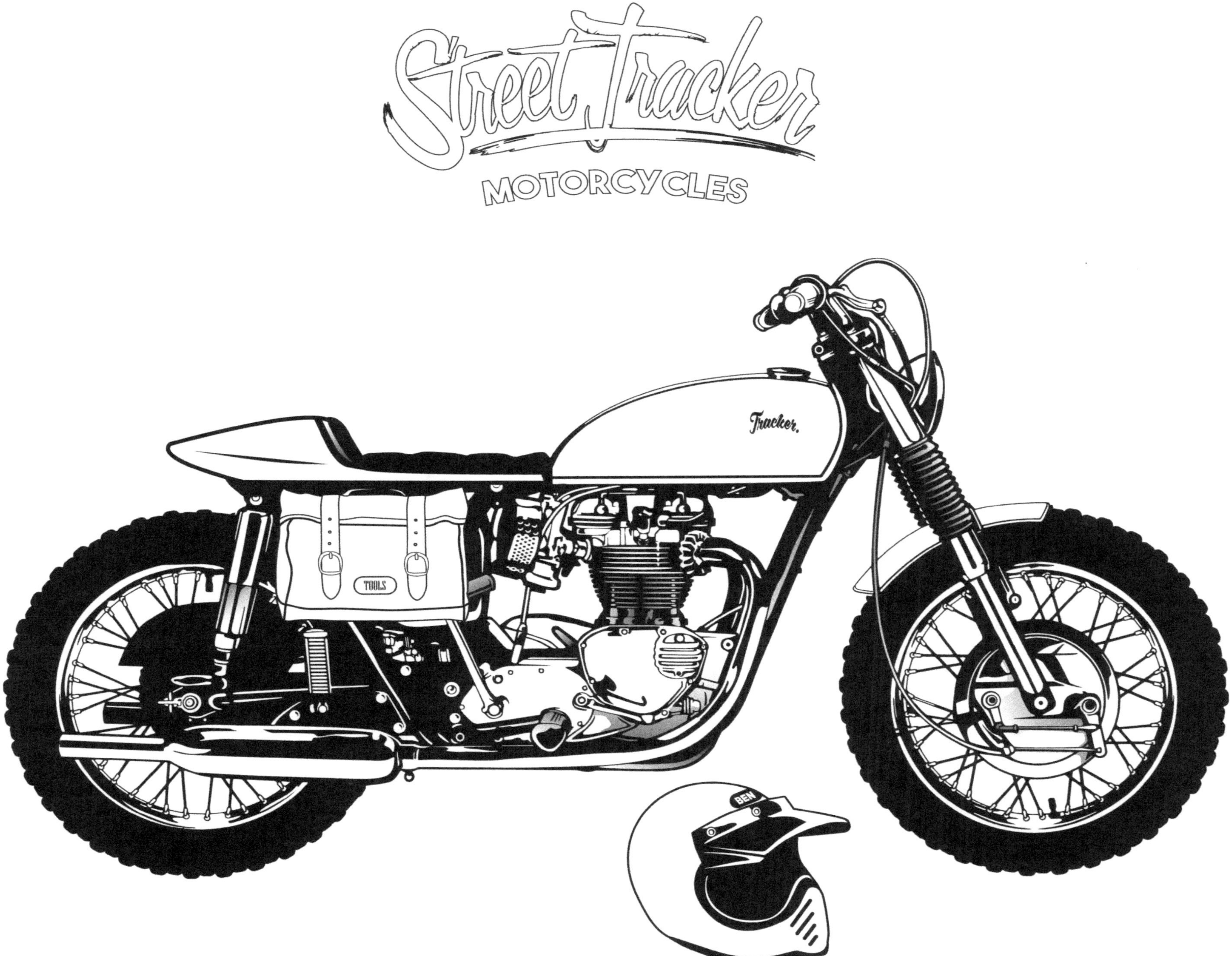